Donald Trump is a Jerk

Donald Trump is a jerk. Donald Trump is a jerk. Donald Trump is a jerk.

By Daniel Alman

Copyright © 2018 Daniel Alman

Table of Contents

Table of Contents continued

About the author

Since there are quite a few people named Daniel Alman in the world, it is worth noting that this particular Daniel Alman was born in 1971, and has spent his entire life so far living in the Squirrel Hill neighborhood of Pittsburgh, Pennsylvania. He has a bachelor's degree in mathematics from the University of Pittsburgh, but even more importantly (at least in his opinion), he attended the Montessori Centre Academy in Glenshaw, Pennsylvania, for ten years, beginning at the age of two.

Mr. Alman ~~thinks~~ knows that Donald Trump is a jerk.

Introduction

Donald Trump is a jerk.

Chapter 1

Donald Trump is a jerk.

Chapter 2

Donald Trump is a jerk.

Donald Trump is a jerk.

Donald Trump is a jerk.

Chapter 3

Donald Trump is a jerk.

Donald Trump is a jerk.

Donald Trump is a jerk.

Donald Trump is a jerk.

Donald Trump is a jerk.

Donald Trump is a jerk.

Donald Trump is a jerk.

Donald Trump is a jerk.

Donald Trump is a jerk.

Donald Trump is a jerk.

Chapter 4

Donald Trump is a jerk. Donald Trump is a jerk.Donald Trump is a jerk. Donald Trump is a jerk. Donald Trump is a jerk.

Chapter 5

Donald Trump is a jerk. Donald Trump is a jerk.Donald Trump is a jerk. Donald Trump is a jerk. Donald Trump is a jerk. Donald Trump

is a jerk. Donald Trump is a jerk.Donald Trump is a jerk. Donald Trump is a jerk. Donald Trump is a jerk. Donald Trump is a jerk. Donald Trump is a jerk. Donald Trump is a jerk. Donald Trump is a jerk. Donald Trump is a jerk. Donald Trump is a jerk. Donald Trump is a jerk. Donald Trump is a jerk. Donald Trump is a jerk.

Donald Trump is a jerk. Donald Trump is a jerk.

Chapter 6

Donald Trump is a jerk. Donald Trump is a jerk.Donald Trump is a jerk. Donald Trump is a jerk. Donald Trump is a jerk. Donald Trump

is a jerk. Donald Trump is a jerk.Donald Trump is a jerk. Donald Trump is a jerk. Donald Trump is a jerk. Donald Trump is a jerk. Donald Trump is a jerk. Donald Trump is a jerk. Donald Trump is a jerk. Donald Trump is a jerk. Donald Trump is a jerk. Donald Trump is a jerk. Donald Trump is a jerk. Donald Trump is a jerk.

Donald Trump is a jerk. Donald

Trump is a jerk. Donald Trump is a jerk.Donald Trump is a jerk. Donald Trump is a jerk. Donald Trump is a jerk. Donald Trump is a jerk. Donald Trump is a jerk. Donald Trump is a jerk. Donald Trump is a jerk. Donald Trump is a jerk. Donald Trump is a jerk. Donald Trump is a jerk. Donald Trump is a jerk. Donald Trump is a jerk. Donald Trump

is a jerk. Donald Trump is a jerk.Donald Trump is a jerk. Donald Trump is a jerk. Donald Trump is a jerk. Donald Trump is a jerk. Donald Trump is a jerk. Donald Trump is a jerk. Donald Trump is a jerk. Donald Trump is a jerk. Donald Trump is a jerk. Donald Trump is a jerk. Donald Trump is a jerk. Donald Trump is a jerk. Donald Trump is a jerk. Donald Trump is a jerk. Donald Trump is a jerk. Donald Trump is a jerk. Donald Trump is a jerk. Donald Trump is a jerk. Donald Trump is a jerk. Donald Trump is a

jerk. Donald Trump is a jerk.

Donald Trump is a jerk. Donald Trump is a jerk.Donald Trump is a jerk. Donald

Trump is a jerk. Donald Trump is a jerk. Donald Trump is a jerk. Donald Trump is a jerk. Donald Trump is a jerk. Donald Trump is a jerk. Donald Trump is a jerk. Donald Trump is a jerk. Donald Trump is a jerk. Donald Trump is a jerk. Donald Trump is a jerk. Donald Trump is a jerk. Donald Trump is a jerk. Donald Trump is a jerk. Donald Trump is a jerk. Donald Trump is a jerk. Donald Trump is a jerk. Donald Trump is a jerk.Donald Trump is a jerk. Donald Trump

is a jerk. Donald Trump is a jerk. Donald
Trump is a jerk. Donald Trump is a jerk.
Donald Trump is a jerk. Donald Trump is a
jerk. Donald Trump is a jerk. Donald Trump
is a jerk. Donald Trump is a jerk. Donald
Trump is a jerk. Donald Trump is a jerk.
Donald Trump is a jerk. Donald Trump is a
jerk. Donald Trump is a jerk. Donald Trump
is a jerk. Donald Trump is a jerk. Donald
Trump is a jerk. Donald Trump is a jerk.
Donald Trump is a jerk. Donald Trump is a
jerk. Donald Trump is a jerk. Donald Trump
is a jerk. Donald Trump is a jerk. Donald
Trump is a jerk. Donald Trump is a jerk.
Donald Trump is a jerk. Donald Trump is a
jerk. Donald Trump is a jerk. Donald Trump
is a jerk. Donald Trump is a jerk. Donald
Trump is a jerk. Donald Trump is a jerk.
Donald Trump is a jerk. Donald Trump is a
jerk. Donald Trump is a jerk. Donald Trump
is a jerk. Donald Trump is a jerk. Donald
Trump is a jerk. Donald Trump is a jerk.
Donald Trump is a jerk. Donald Trump is a

jerk. Donald Trump is a jerk. Donald Trump is a jerk. Donald Trump is a jerk. Donald Trump is a jerk. Donald Trump is a jerk. Donald Trump is a jerk. Donald Trump is a jerk. Donald Trump is a jerk. Donald Trump is a jerk. Donald Trump is a jerk. Donald Trump is a jerk. Donald Trump is a jerk. Donald Trump is a jerk. Donald Trump is a jerk. Donald Trump is a jerk.Donald Trump is a jerk. Donald Trump is a jerk.

Donald Trump is a jerk. Donald Trump is a jerk. Donald Trump is a jerk. Donald Trump is a jerk. Donald Trump is a jerk. Donald Trump is a jerk. Donald Trump is a jerk. Donald Trump is a jerk.Donald Trump is a jerk. Donald Trump is a jerk. Donald Trump is a jerk. Donald Trump is a jerk. Donald Trump is a jerk. Donald Trump is a jerk. Donald Trump is a jerk. Donald Trump is a jerk. Donald Trump is a jerk. Donald Trump is a jerk. Donald Trump is a jerk. Donald Trump is a jerk. Donald Trump is a jerk. Donald Trump is a jerk. Donald Trump is a jerk. Donald Trump is a jerk. Donald Trump is a jerk.

Chapter 7

Donald Trump is a jerk.

Chapter 8

Donald Trump is a jerk. Donald Trump is a jerk.Donald Trump is a jerk. Donald Trump is a jerk. Donald Trump is a jerk. Donald Trump

is a jerk. Donald Trump is a jerk.Donald Trump is a jerk. Donald Trump is a jerk. Donald Trump is a jerk. Donald Trump is a jerk. Donald Trump is a jerk. Donald Trump is a jerk. Donald Trump is a jerk. Donald Trump is a jerk. Donald Trump is a jerk. Donald Trump is a jerk. Donald Trump is a jerk. Donald Trump is a jerk. Donald Trump is a jerk.

Donald Trump is a jerk. Donald

Trump is a jerk. Donald Trump is a jerk.Donald Trump is a jerk. Donald Trump is a jerk. Donald Trump is a jerk. Donald Trump is a jerk. Donald Trump is a jerk. Donald Trump is a jerk. Donald Trump is a jerk. Donald Trump is a jerk. Donald Trump is a jerk. Donald Trump is a jerk. Donald Trump

is a jerk. Donald Trump is a

jerk. Donald Trump is a jerk. Donald Trump is a jerk. Donald Trump is a jerk. Donald Trump is a jerk. Donald Trump is a jerk. Donald Trump is a jerk. Donald Trump is a jerk. Donald Trump is a jerk. Donald Trump is a jerk. Donald Trump is a jerk.Donald Trump is a jerk. Donald Trump is a jerk.

Donald Trump is a jerk.Donald Trump is a jerk. Donald Trump is a jerk.

Chapter 9

Donald Trump is a jerk.

Donald Trump is a jerk.

Donald Trump is a jerk.

Donald Trump is a jerk.

Donald Trump is a jerk.

Conclusion

Donald Trump is a jerk.